TAOS TALES

Alexander Boeringa

TAOS TALES

Alexander Boeringa

TAOS TALES

Cover art is from a painting by Herman Rednick, who was a Taos artist, spiritual leader and friend.

Disclaimer: Some names have been changed to protect the privacy of individuals.

Alexander Boeringa is also the author of *Opening a Closed Door: A Psychotherapist Remembers His Patients*.

Contents

TAOS TALES

INTRODUCTION

I was not born a Taoseño, but as some might say, "I got there as soon as I could." Despite many moves since I first lived there, it was my spiritual home and it always will be. The time I spent in Northern New Mexico totally reformed and influenced my life. I still think of people and events from this period, and I sometimes wake up in the morning knowing that I have been dreaming about something that happened many years ago. Then I might forget about my life in Taos for weeks or even months. But one morning not long ago, "for no good reason" I woke up with my head totally filled with thoughts of Taos. I immediately knew that I had to write these memories down and share them. I tried to think of a way to tell the stories so they could be read in order, but they still seemed to be jumbled up. I thought of many different ways to organize my memories. Then I just began.

This book is not a tourist guide, and it is not a list of "must-see" places. Instead, it is about my life and my love affair with Taos. I want to share with you what is unique about Taos. I lived here, this is what I did, this is what impressed me, and these are my thoughts.

Wherever I have lived, I have tried to fit in with the people who are already there. They were there before I arrived; it is I who must adjust to their way of life. This includes getting to know my neighbors, respecting them, honoring their history and customs as best I can, and maybe even learning a little of their language. Somewhat selfishly, I am the one who reaps the most benefit from this approach; I think you will too.

Whether you are reading this book during your first visit to Taos or if you live here, I hope you will find information that will inspire you to explore and create your own memories. I learned some things about accessing a culture when I first moved to Taos, and these have often helped me as I have moved throughout the world. Perhaps they will be useful to you as well.

The best suggestion is to skip the tourist trail and just walk around and talk to people who look interesting and approachable to you. After the first "Now what does this person want…" skeptical look from them, I bet that both of you will be glad you met. Many people love where they live and enjoy sharing it with others.

Another suggestion is to read books or watch movies about Taos, such as *The Milagro Beanfield War*. They provide a charming introduction to New Mexico and some of its people. I recognized each of the characters in that book. Not that I personally knew each one, but many of them reminded me of the real-life people I have known and still care about.

Finally, just so you know: This book follows a recipe. Here is how I concocted *Taos Tales*:

- Take the 100% truth about Taos
- Mix in a little "artistic license"
- Add a bit of outright lies
- Mix well and serve.

You decide how much of each of the ingredients are in each serving. I honestly don't know. All I can say is that they have been well mixed in my own memory, and I believe each word that is written here.

So grab a Taos tale and drink up.

HOME

Many years ago, I left my home in Austin, Texas, late at night, and drove until the next morning. The last part of the trip was on the low road from Santa Fe and along the beautiful Rio Grande River. As I topped Pilar Hill, I saw my new home, new adventures, and a new life spread out below me. I had visited Taos before and it had long been my dream to move there. Now I knew that I was home.

Now please back up a day to Monday morning in Austin.

I did not care much for my job and was saving my money so that I could quit and move to Taos. I dreaded going to work on Mondays because there was always a staff meeting and a haranguing about something by management. This Monday was to be different. We were all seated, drinking our morning coffee and wondering what could possibly have gone wrong this time. In walked the big boss, no "Good morning," no eye contact, he just said, "This place is out of business. You can collect your last paychecks on the way out." And he quickly left. That was it. This was not the first time my employment so suddenly shifted through no fault of my own; and as you will read later, it was not the last time.

Now, we can return to Tuesday.

As I looked down at the town below, every item I owned was either on my body or in the saddlebags of the motorcycle I was sitting on. I was happy. Thanks to the help of some friends, I found an apartment I could rent by the end of the day, and I had an offer of some "good hard work in the broiling sun for minimum wages." I was home.

OMG! ISN'T THAT...?

The rich and famous have been coming to the Taos area for a long time now, but the influx swelled considerably in the late 1960s. It was probably good for the high-end real estate economy, but not for many of the people who lived there. My experience is that, for the most part, the locals had never heard of some of the newcomers, or if they had, they did not care. They only saw their taxes go up, and sometimes even their land sold out from under them to pay off their debts.

The *Easy Rider* movie was partially filmed in and around Taos and, as I rode a motorcycle, I was especially interested in seeing where some of the scenes had been shot. This was not hard to do, as many of the people involved were excited to share some of their experiences with me. For example, the opening was filmed on the road leading to the house of someone I knew. He loved to tell the story of how exciting it was to have the movie crew around and to see the stars in person. The locals even earned a little money for the use of their property.

Celebrities who lived in or visited Taos always caused quite a stir but it was considered very "un-cool" to intrude upon their privacy. Still, people surreptitiously followed them down the street or around the aisles of the grocery store. Robert Redford bought property in Taos, and Bob Dylan was often sighted on the streets. There were many others, less famous but equally interesting.

One lady was frequently seen walking around wearing a long, sweeping dress and a few thousand dollars' worth of Indian jewelry. Some said she was a local; others swore that they recognized her and wasn't she…oh you know…that star in that movie…?

A local resident, whose family was well known in California social circles, had inherited millions. He lived simply and never showed off, except I once heard him refer to a million-dollar lawsuit against him as "people trying to nickel and dime him to death." I sometimes drank coffee with his accountant, who told me one morning that he calculated that if this man tried to spend the interest on his money by passing it out on the street, he would have to give away ten dollars a minute for eight hours a day, every weekday, all year long. I did not know the man of whom the accountant spoke, but I did once install a toilet in his house. He came by, introduced himself, and we talked for a while. Before he left, he reminded me to be sure to put a brick in the tank to conserve water. He was in many respects a "regular person" who avoided publicity. He was not the only rich person in town. A few others I met looked like hippies, and they fit in well with the local culture. Come to think of it, I too looked pretty much like a hippie at the time, but I certainly was not rich.

Another millionaire I knew lived in a converted chicken coop for a while, but not for long. I think he soon purchased several acres on the top of a nearby mountain. The dirt road leading to it was so bad that at its beginning there was a sign, "Pick your rut carefully, you will be in it for the next nine miles." There was a rumor circulating that before retiring to his "hermithood" at the end of the road, he left a friend with enough money to buy land and establish yet another hippie commune.

Many of the young people I knew were like me, often from a middle-class family, not poor, fairly well to very well educated, and all looking for a different kind of life than our parents had. Most of us tried different "recreational drugs," but didn't get caught up in them to the point of addiction. Many of the hippies eventually married and raised families, yet continued to maintain an alternate lifestyle. In general, they probably fit quite well in today's more relaxed society. One of them even became a clinical psychologist, who now enjoys his children and grandchildren...none of whom are hippies.

LOCAL ART

While walking around town one day, I came upon a man on the top rungs of a rickety stepladder, sawing away at one of the extended roof beams of a house. These round logs, called *vigas*, are trees stripped of the bark by hand and left to dry for a season or two before being used as supports for a roof. They usually have the ends cut with an axe into "pencil points" giving them an especially rustic look. For some reason, after these *vigas* probably had been there for several hundred years, this man decided to trim them. He had already cut the ends off one or two vigas to make them flat and considerably shorter.

Taos being a small town, I stopped to chat with him, and we agreed that, yes, it was a hot day and the work did look exhausting. In the course of our friendly conversation, I asked him why he was trimming the vigas. He said that he thought they looked "neater" with the ends cut off. I ventured the opinion that they looked better with their original ends, more authentic so to speak. He climbed down from the ladder, looked up at them, and said that, yes, now that I mentioned it, he thought so too. He immediately folded his ladder, thanked me, and walked away.

The several remaining *vigas* were left in their original state, and the one he had been working on was only half-sawn through. And so they stayed, unless some

compulsive sort has come along and "made them even."
Since then, I have enjoyed walking past that building
when I've been in Taos, and have admired the results of
my intervention. I was amused by my part in it, and I
admired the man not only for being able to change his
mind, but to take such decisive action as well.

Taoseños are deservedly proud of the wonderful
silver and turquoise jewelry created there. It happened
from time to time that some local artisan would stop by my
house, or meet me on the street, and ask if I wanted to
buy a belt buckle. What I was shown was always quite
beautiful and the price was much lower than I would have
had to pay in the shops. Unfortunately, I was never able
to buy any because I could not afford them. The purchase
of one buckle would have cost me a week or two of meals.
I later realized that by not being able to sell something,
the man's entire family might have gone hungry for a
while. These were hard times for many people who,
having lived here for centuries, were now being squeezed
out by taxes, the rising cost of living, and lack of work in
Taos.

I built a home later when I had a job and a little
money. I needed a fireplace in it, and I wanted it to be in
the Taos style of adobe and with gentle curves. I learned
that one of the things my ex-landlady Carmen did was to
make wonderfully sculpted adobe fireplaces for people. I
asked her, and she agreed to build one for me. I
remember she looked carefully at the room and then
asked me where I wanted the fireplace placed, how large,
and whether I wanted a small recessed shelf, or *nicho*,
above it. Then she told me to get out and let her work, and

not to come back until she told me it was finished. When I finally did see it completed, I was very happy. It was a true work of art.

When I first came to Taos, it was comprised of several groups of people. In the order of arrival, there were the Taos Indian pueblo dwellers, then came the Spanish, and soon the Anglos in general, and the many artists in particular. I arrived with the influx of hippies. Then there were the skiers. And always, of course, there were the tourists.

ADOBE

The most common and picturesque sites in New Mexico are the adobe buildings. I lived in an adobe home at one time and loved it. I also built with adobe and hated it. I hated it because of the hard work, but I found it worth the effort. Anyone who owns or has ever lived in an adobe can tell you how well they fit the needs of their environment. They are cool in the summer, warm in the winter, blend beautifully with the prevailing arid landscape, and are made of what is potentially the least expensive building material available. I say potentially because, although they consist of readily available materials (dirt, straw, and stone), assembly is very labor-intensive. Elsewhere in this book, I mention that to build with adobe you probably have to be either very rich or very poor.

Let's begin with the adobe bricks. They are constructed with mud and straw, mixed with enough water to mold well and dry strong. Churning the mixture with your feet is very hard work. A day of this may feel like it is either killing you or making you stronger. I have made bricks on a small scale and I hope never to do it again.

After churning the mixture, you put it into molds to partially dry until it is able to maintain its form. You then remove the blocks and let them age in the sun. Next, you carry them to the building site, which is hopefully nearby, and begin stacking them to make a wall. As walls go up, they require even more lifting, bending, and carrying. Bear in mind that each brick probably weighs between twenty-five and thirty-five pounds, depending on the size you want. Most bricks for house walls are 4" x 8" x 12", but they can be thicker and proportionately heavier. (Larger flat bricks will be used eventually for construction of the roof.) The bricks are plastered into place with more adobe mud.

Once the walls are up, the roof beams can be laid. These are called *vigas* and, hopefully, they will come from nearby tall, straight trees that have been felled, barked and left for a season to dry. Consider: How wide do you want your rooms to be? How many friends do you have to lift these *vigas* to the height of your roof? Thinner branches of wood, called *latillas*, are placed on top of the vigas, and mud and brush are repeatedly added to form the roof.

Spaces are left in the walls for doors and windows. The windows are generally small: large enough to let some light in, but not so big as to compromise the benefit of thick walls in maintaining temperature. Another reason for small windows was that the early settlers didn't want to provide easy access by enemies.

If you are able to visit an adobe home, do so. You will see how cleverly this most fluid of materials has also been put to good use in interior walls. Gentle curves, especially above doorways, are common. While there might be pictures on the wall, you are more likely to see several *nichos* on which small treasures are displayed.

I wrote earlier about the beautiful and artistic fireplace that Carmen built for me. A clay fireplace can be as wonderful and as diverse as the artists who built them. My fireplace always drew as well as or better than any in which I have built a fire. Since they are used to actually heat a space, as well as being decorative, the builders are experts in making sure that they function perfectly. My current home has a "fireplace," yet I have never bothered to light the artificial gas logs and I doubt I ever will. Yes, these can be "cozy," but I would always be comparing it with a Taos fireplace.

Have you ever wondered why adobe houses have ladders leaning against them? It is because, although it seldom rains enough to hurt the adobe, melting snow can be a problem. You need to get up on the roof and remove the snow before it accumulates and begins to melt. Otherwise, the water would sink down between your roof layers and drip on your head. This is an early warning system that tells you it is time to get up on the roof with a shovel.

Because adobe homes are vulnerable to the infrequent rains of summer and the sometimes harsh snows of winter, exterior surfaces need to be repaired periodically. To accomplish this, fresh mud is smoothed over the cracks and holes. A coat of paint may be applied to delay the aging process. For those who can afford it, an easier, more permanent method is to cover the adobe with concrete plaster that has the desired color already mixed in. This theoretically lasts "forever." In fact, many of the newer "adobe" houses you will see are probably made entirely with cement that has been colored to look like adobe. Sometimes people plaster ornamental features into the walls. I have seen many very creative designs using bits of glass or other decorative objects. Look for these as you wander around town. Later in this book, you will read about my own plastering experiences.

FITTING IN WITH THE COMMUNITY

For a long time, Randall's was the only large lumberyard in Taos. It was the place to meet friends, especially other construction workers; to find out how work was going; and to talk about the weather. The owner mostly hired Indian men from the pueblo to serve the customers. They did things the old way, and often used hand saws to cut lumber even though the store obviously sold electric skill saws. I never thought to ask them why they chose to use handsaws. Perhaps it was because of tradition, or perhaps dragging electrical cords around was a nuisance. I wonder if they still choose the hand tools.

I once encountered an interesting racial cliché spoken by one of the Indian staff. I had called the store one morning and asked the clerk if a man named Tom had been by, or if he was currently in the store, as I wanted to talk with him. The clerk said he did not know him. I knew that Tom was often in the store, sometimes at least once a day, so I found this surprising. I proceeded to describe him. Again, the clerk answered that he didn't know him. Later that day I saw Tom. He told me that he was in the store at the time I had called. In fact, he thought that he had been waited on by the same clerk I spoke with.

I needed to buy some things at the lumber yard that afternoon, and I was curious about what had occurred. I talked to the same clerk and again gave a description of Tom. At this point, the man just looked at me, and with a straight face said: "I don't know; all white men look alike to me."

I THINK I was being had, but I still am not really sure.

Another time I was telling a friend about a specific dimension of lumber that was sometimes difficult to obtain. I needed a few pieces of these boards and I was going to Randall's to buy them. My friend told me to forget it since he needed the same size lumber and was told on the phone that morning that it was not in stock. Later that same afternoon, I was in the store buying something else, and I saw a huge stack of the exact size. I pulled out what I needed and when I was checking out, I asked the clerk if they had just received a load of it. He said no, the lumber had been there all week. I asked him why he had told my friend that they didn't have any. Without a smile, he answered, "I don't like him."

I was happy to be living in Taos but I could not survive there unless I periodically found work. Permanent employment was almost impossible to find, and my rent and food did not come cheap. One lucky break came when my friend Guilford hired me to work on a place he was building in the village of San Cristobal. As a generous bonus, he offered me the use of a house he owned. It was a large adobe and was well insulated by thick walls, but, of course, the fireplace was its only source of heat. I could not heat the whole house; it was too big. I was told I would need to cut enough wood to fill the room I wanted to live and sleep in. I had a chain saw, a truck, enough time and determination, but I never did meet the goal of having enough wood. Not even close. Fortunately, I never froze.

Of course, all of my neighbors were in the same situation, so we spent a lot of spare time in the mountains cutting wood for the winter. The Forest Service helped out in its own way by "chaining" parts of the land it administered. In order to open up the forest for grazing or provide roads or firebreaks, it would put two huge bulldozers side by side with a logging chain between them and just knock down everything that got in the way. The timber lying on the ground was available for use by anyone.

The amount of gas and the time it took to drive up the mountain and back made it tempting to overload the beat-up and overburdened pickup trucks most of us drove. You could see their compressed springs and squashed-down tires, and hear the groans from every other part as they were slowly driven down the rutted dirt roads toward home. Every time they swayed, they appeared ready to topple over or to have the top logs fall off. Breakdowns were not uncommon.

One day one of these old trucks laden with way too much wood broke down right in front of my house. I offered the Spanish driver help to secure the truck, and we waited for his friends to arrive. I shared a cup of coffee with him in the kitchen. We had a pleasant talk about the usual things, such as the weather, the price of alfalfa, and a little gossip about the village. Since I was both a newcomer and an Anglo, he asked about me also, so I shared a little of my history and told him what I was doing there. He, of course, knew my friend Guilford, who had lived in the valley for several years. Guilford was generally well-liked by the long-term inhabitants, most of whom were also Spanish. Note that I say Spanish and not Mexican. The people living in Taos traced their lineage directly back to old Spain. When later I lived briefly in the Andalucía region of Spain, I encountered many of the same names that occurred in Taos.

What I did not know at the time was that this man was a very highly respected leader in the community. It was also an indisputable fact that, in general, he was known not to care much for Anglos. He especially did not like those who bought up land his people had lived on for hundreds of years. Most often the sellers were poor Spanish people whose families owned little else. Now they had to sell it and move. At least I had never mentioned to my guest that I previously lived in Texas; those buyers came in for special disdain. Bumper stickers reading "Texans Go Home" were common.

My meeting with this man and the friends who came to help him went well. However, unloading and reloading the wood from his truck was hard work, and the sun was hot. I offered beer. I think that action influenced my future relations with "the locals" in a very positive manner.

WATER IN THE VALLEY

Agriculture in the San Cristobal Valley has always depended on irrigation water. The water flows down from the snowmelt in the adjacent Sangre de Cristo Mountains through ditches of the *Acequia Madre*. These ditches have to be cleaned and maintained each spring, and when I lived in the valley, the men of the village would gather to do this task. Most of the Anglo residents did not help with the work, but instead would pay some young Spanish boy to show up at the work call to do their share. However, I wanted to be part of the community, so I showed up on the appointed day, with my shovel and straw hat, ready to do my part. Small groups of men stood together in clumps talking, and it was obvious that they took note of my presence, but I did not know anyone well enough to join a group without being asked. So, I stood apart feeling quite the outsider and waiting to be told what to do.

The man I once helped with his truckload of wood recognized me and whispered something to the men around him. I assume he was telling them that I had recently assisted him. Since he was one of the lead men in the village, his word clearly carried weight. His message circulated, and soon a man separated himself from one of the groups, came over, introduced himself and invited me to join his crew.

The work was really quite easy; a few people could have done it by themselves if necessary. I think, though, that the real point of being together was to reaffirm the local culture and values, and to catch up on the winter's news. It was a rite of spring. Whenever we passed near someone's land, the owner would invite us all to have a drink of water from his well. I noticed that it was good form to comment on how pure and refreshing the water was. It was equally important to listen to the story of the well: when it was dug, and how it had never gone dry, even in "that bad spell a few years back." At the end of the day, I felt marginally accepted, still an outsider as I always would be, but tolerated.

Water being such an important and precious commodity in the valley, it was carefully guarded. If the *majordomo* (or water boss) granted two hours of irrigation for my field starting at 2 a.m. and I wanted water, I had better take it then. Right on the hour, I would turn the water through the water gate into my ditch. I would make sure it ran well and was not blocked, overflowing, or running down a gopher hole into my neighbor's field. Moreover, I needed to turn the water back into the main ditch before 4 a.m. Fights, sometimes involving shovels, over infringements or stealing water were not unheard of here. Extra water might provide an additional cutting of alfalfa, which in turn, might determine whether there would be enough food on the table, and whether the children got new shoes for the school year. For more insight about water rights in a rural community, I again recommend the book and movie, *The Milagro Beanfield War*. The movie was actually shot in Truchas, New

Mexico, halfway between Santa Fe and Taos. It was based on the book of the same title, and written by John Nichols.

When a water board meeting was held one night at the local schoolhouse, I went and sat in the back. Much of the meeting was routine, boring business. It was conducted in English, but many of the comments or asides were made in Spanish. I went because I wanted to be as much a part of this community as it would allow, even though I would always be an Anglo and an outsider. I wanted to be accepted at least as a neighbor and, hopefully, as a friend.

After the reading of the previous month's minutes, a call was made for the election of a new president, and the chairman requested nominations. For the first time all evening, there were long minutes of total silence. No one looked at anyone else. We sat. Finally, one man slowly stood up and said that he nominated Raúl. Then he slowly sat down. Again, we waited. A few minutes later, another man stood and seconded the nomination. We sat. The chairman finally asked if anyone wished to add other names. No response. So he then decreed that Raúl was chosen, and asked for a show of hands by all those in favor of this candidate. Hands slowly went up, and then slowly went down. By a majority vote, Raúl was acclaimed the next president.

At this point, Raúl stood up and said in a quiet voice, "I don't think I want to do it," and then sat down again. Another candidate was not nominated that evening, but I am sure that things were eventually worked out.

My well usually produced good water. It was a dug well, about twenty-five feet deep, and the walls were lined with brick. It was covered with a metal lid, and on top there was an electric pump to lift the water and pipe it to the house. However, one day the water was foul. An animal had somehow gotten into the well and drowned. I was able to fish the putrefying carcass out using a bucket, but it was not a pleasant task. I then carefully followed the directions of the county agricultural agent, and pumped the entire well dry. As new water slowly seeped back in, I poured bleach into the water and let it sit for a few days. I again pumped the well dry, and repeated the process once more. After a week, the new water was supposed to be potable. However, I continued to boil it for the next few weeks. The water felt strange, even when I was only bathing in it.

There was a wonderful continuity to living in Taos that seemed to mirror all of life. In the winter it snowed, and one could see the snowcap up on Grandfather Mountain. In the spring one could see the small streams running down the mountainside, the irrigated fields, the scattered wells, and close by, the Rio Grande River at the bottom of a deep canyon. I felt very close to nature and to the earth. Since I was living in an adobe house, I was even surrounded by the earth, literally from floor to ceiling. I have never before, or after, felt like I was living so close to nature, and so touched by her.

GOOD NEIGHBORS

My closest neighbor was a family with two young children, and the kids liked to come by and visit. I suppose I provided a break from the other adults in their lives. The boy enjoyed helping me in the garden, and after I introduced him to eating raw sugar peas, he broadcast this information to every other child in the area. I soon found that all of the peas had been consumed and I was being asked what else was good to eat.

The boy didn't have a dog, but he loved playing catch and tug-of-war with my dog, Rama. The little girl was very cute, knew it, and played on this advantage at every opportunity that presented itself. Once she discovered that I was generous with the cookies, she visited almost every day. Hiding the cookie tin only slowed her down, and she made a coquettish game of talking me out of the hiding place.

One day she came over and told me that it was her birthday. I hurriedly rushed out to buy her a few small presents, and showed up at her house at the time she said the party was to begin. At first, there was some odd family activity, only to be told by her confused parents that her birthday was actually five months off. The girl hid her face and then smiled unabashedly, and we all laughed together and were served a piece of non-birthday cake. It was the first of many pleasant meals with this family.

I should mention here that I am a vegetarian, a fact that sometimes confused many of the people I met. Most of them had never encountered this concept before, and for them, meat was often a luxury, so they had a difficult time trying to figure me out. I think some of them just put it down to my being an Anglo, and they already knew how strange we could be. Most, however, somehow rose to the occasion, but I have eaten way more than my share of overcooked and soggy vegetables. I always met my hosts' kindnesses with earnest protestations of how delicious the food was and that, no, I was not still hungry.

I had my own horses for a while. Here's how this came to be. I was building a fence around the field I owned. A local man I knew named Hipolito was helping me dig postholes and string barbed wire. Then he asked me why I wanted to fence the land. I said I was thinking of buying a couple of horses to ride. At this, he launched into a long, and I thought unnecessary, diatribe about why this was such a bad idea, how much horses cost to buy and keep, and on and on. It began to annoy me; after all, what business of his was it?

I went shopping on the next Saturday morning, and when I returned home there were two horses in my yard. They had bridles on them and the saddles were perched on a nearby rail fence. No note, no call, just the horses. I called Hipolito to thank him and he said, "Oh well, I have several horses and I do not use them very often," and added that I could keep them as long as I liked.

One of the horses was my favorite, and I rode him most often. If I was going to ride outside the field or around town, he was glad to oblige. He seemed to enjoy the leisurely rides and the opportunity to visit other horses along the way. But if I tried to ride him around the several-acre pasture only for exercise, he would balk and almost always try to throw me. Independent he was.

The other horse was so gentle that I could ride her with just a blanket, and guide her with my knees. She always plodded along and seemed happy with just my company. I often rode around Taos, sometimes to run an errand or to visit friends like Samuel. On the other hand, another of my neighbors had a semi-retired thoroughbred racehorse. It was retired only in the sense that it was no longer raced at the track. Left to its own, it clearly loved to run, but it was very fast, temperamental, and difficult to control. My neighbor once asked me if I wanted to ride him. No, thank you. I am best suited for plodding.

One of the things that I most enjoyed about the time I spent with my neighbors was hearing their stories about families staying together for generations. Despite some changes in lifestyle, many of them clung to traditional values and the old way of doing things. For example, a friend once told me that his mother did all of her baking and cooking with an ancient wood stove that she had used as long as any of them could remember. As she was getting older, they thought she would appreciate not having to get up early to chop and carry wood and start the fire. So for her birthday, the whole family chipped in to buy a new gas stove for her. He said she beamed when she saw all the painted metal and chrome of the new stove, but within a week she was back to using the old one. As a concession to their kindness, however, she did admit that she really liked using the new one for reheating coffee. I have since heard similar stories involving microwave ovens.

SAMUEL – PART I

Samuel was a lean, well-weathered old man with a beautiful soul, what in Spanish is called an "*alma de Dios.*" He did various odd jobs around town. I first met him when I worked alongside him, plastering a house. On this, my first job with Samuel, I was the least skilled on the two-man crew, and it was my task to prepare the basic plaster and add the correct amount of color to the cement. Fortunately, I was able to use an electric cement mixer rather than a trough to prepare the mix. But I still had to stagger over rough ground with the bags of cement, dump them in the mixer, add just the right amount of water, and get the color exactly right. Samuel was very clear about this; if the mixture was not the consistency he needed, he would reject it. Once, I think it was just to teach me a lesson, he dumped what I handed him, and told me to redo the batch. Samuel was a very fast worker, and sometimes it was difficult to keep up with him. Shoveling and mixing was demanding work; plus, I had to transport the heavy sludge in a wheelbarrow, up inclined planks without spilling too much. Losing an entire load in the dirt was unthinkable.

One day when I looked at the wall he was plastering, I noticed a few oddly shaped and slightly darker variations in the light-yellow hue. I pointed this out to Samuel and asked if there was a reason. He looked at me for a long moment as if this was just the kind of question a dumb Anglo would ask. He then turned and spit a fine stream of tobacco juice onto the wet plaster and with a smile on his face blended it in with his trowel. Later that day, I was sent to buy a fresh plug of tobacco. Naturally, before quitting at the end of a long day, I had to wash and put away all of the equipment, coil the hoses, clean up the site, and have supplies ready for the next day. He, of course, was the maestro so he got to go home. Samuel came to me as he was leaving on that day. Grinning, he handed me his trowel and patted me on the back. When I looked up, I saw that he had left a particularly dark swirl in the area where he last worked.

I once was asked by someone to build a nice-looking wall along their property, but only if I could do it for a "fair" price. The mention of "fair," of course, meant "cheap." This man, from somewhere in Texas, had little idea of what went into building anything, but since he was rich, he thought he knew everything. He wanted "a strong wall, one that would last." To this end, he specified that it would have "posts" of stacked cinder blocks every so often, and we were to put reinforcing iron bars and cement in them. I told him this was unnecessary but he insisted.

I needed the money, so I made a bid as low as I could to cover the labor and materials, and he accepted. He paid half and said that he would be back in a week to see how it looked and then pay me the other half of my money. I told a good friend of mine that I would be building this wall and explained filling the "interstitial porosities", a term he still jokes with me about to this day. What he actually said was, "Only an overeducated pretender like you could use a line like that."

There was a lot of work to do, so I asked Samuel to help me. He was, as they say, "between jobs" and we were glad to be working together again. When I explained the interstitial porosities thing to him, he kind of snorted and said that was the silliest thing he had ever heard of. We left it at that for the moment. As usual, we worked quite well together, and had nearly completed the block work; now it was time to fill the holes. I had something to do the next morning, but I planned to buy the rebar and extra cement after that. On the way to the store, I stopped by the job to see if Samuel wanted to go with me. It was then that I noticed that all of the posts were already finished and nicely capped with cement. "What happened here, Samuel? Did you get everything together yourself and work all night?"

"Nooo," he drew out in his typical slow response. "I just filled those holes with broken bits of rock and things and poured the cement on top. It didn't take very long, and it's just as good as that other stupid thing. And it sure saves us money." "Uh-oh," I thought, "What now?" "But Samuel", I said, "we promised we would put rebar and cement in those holes!" "Well," he slyly added, "you know those old pieces of metal lying around? I put them in there, too, and a little wet cement. It's reinforced, so we didn't lie." What was I to do? Besides, Samuel was right in a way, and the last time I went to look, that wall and those posts were still there and looking good.

I had, and I retain, a great deal of affection for Samuel. I liked to ride my horse to his house to visit him and his wife. We would have coffee together and he would tell me stories about his early life. Once, he volunteered to go up in the mountains with me on horseback to show me where he had roamed as a boy, and to take me to the places he knew. He said he could even point to the area where, as legend had it, outlaw gold was buried. We never did make the trip, and I am sorry to this day that I did not make the time for it. It was my loss.

I learned a great deal from Samuel about life in general, life in Taos, and how to be a good friend, which he was.

SAMUEL – PART II

I loved working for and with Samuel. As we worked together on plastering and other jobs, we always talked, usually quite a bit. He was full of stories, and I was full of curiosity. He came from a large family and had many relatives in the area. One of his best tales was about an uncle who had died. This man was an Army veteran and it was well known to the entire community that he received a monthly government pension check. After picking it up at the post office, he would go to the bank, cash the check, and go home. He owned a very small, two-room adobe hut out in the middle of a field. He had his own garden, ate simply, and did not drink. Since he had few expenses, there was much speculation by the townspeople about what he did with "all that money." Kids, evidently including Samuel, at times snuck around his house to spy on him. They all reported that he had a Mason jar that he kept on a shelf above the wood stove, and that each time he returned from the bank, he would empty his newest riches into it. You can imagine, in a small community like Taos, how quickly this story circulated.

With time, the legend grew that he had filled many Mason jars over the years and, naturally, curiosity centered on what he did with them. Inevitably, a myth developed that he must have hidden all of the jars. Here was the lure of buried treasure. What could be more enticing for gossip, and offer encouragement for further wild exaggeration? The years passed, and eventually so did the old man. Samuel was the closest surviving relative and was known to have inherited the property. (Need I explain that everyone in town made it their business to know everyone else's business?)

Samuel told me that within hours of the word getting around about his uncle's death, his own nephew came to visit him. After commenting on the high cost of funerals these days, he "mentioned" how unfair it was that his favorite uncle had been left to bear the expense all alone. He then said that he might be willing to help Samuel pay the cost. Receiving no reply, he continued by saying that since he had a good job and could afford it better than Samuel, it was only right that he should pay the whole cost. And, he continued, all he wanted in return was the use of the field his dear great-uncle had owned and, of course, the almost worthless adobe. Samuel somewhat reluctantly agreed and the nephew planned a fitting, but not too expensive, burial with a nice, but not elaborate, headstone. For all of this, Samuel's nephew paid. Then he moved his sheep onto the land and, naturally, he had to visit them frequently to feed and water the animals.

At this point in the story, Samuel smiled broadly and said that he visited the old adobe one evening a few weeks after the funeral. He noticed that several shallow holes had been dug in and around the house. In addition, a hollow tree had been cut into, and a stone fence had been partially demolished. He looked carefully at me to make sure I understood. Then with a grin, he went on to say that after another two weeks had passed, he heard that his nephew had rented a jackhammer. Thereafter, the sound of it could be heard on weekends and, bit by bit, the hut was essentially reduced to rubble. The surrounding ground was pocketed by holes, and another tree had been uprooted.

Obviously, I was meant to ask him the inevitable question, and Samuel waited patiently for me to do so, and so I bit: "Did he ever find the buried treasure?" "Nooo," he slowly said, then paused for a long moment and continued, "There was not much money there anyway; less than a hundred dollars. I went to the house as soon as I heard that my uncle died. The money was all on the shelf." A slow count of ten, and then Samuel slapped his knees with delight and roared with laughter. He seemed to equally savor the remembrance of his nephew paying for the funeral, and of all his fruitless hard work with the pick, shovel, and jackhammer. My own laughter joined with his. I both enjoyed the story and clearly showed appropriate respect for the cleverness I knew that Samuel felt was his due.

I am sure his nephew was not amused, though, when Samuel now and again slowly leaked bits and pieces of the history to a trusted gossip or two. And certainly, the town, being the town, soon knew the whole story from beginning to end, and took great delight in bringing the subject up whenever they had the chance to do so, especially when the nephew was within earshot.

WHATEVER WORKS

These stories cover several years and a lot of territory. I was very poor when I arrived in Taos. Financial necessity led me to learn many "occupations." One was plumbing.

I did not know much about plumbing at first, but I quickly learned. It also helped that I sometimes worked with a man who had been a plumber all of his life. He knew everything about how to actually do the work, but he never held a license because he could not pass the exam. Because I could read, memorize, and pass tests, I eventually obtained a master's level plumbing license. I had the license and could sign off on permit applications; he knew how to finish the job. Together we made quite a team.

When I first started, though, I often did projects I had never done before, some of them "on the fly," as they say. For example, once a man asked me if I could install a septic tank. I had never built one before, but I confidently told him, "Of course, I can! When do you want it put in?" He then replied, "Is tomorrow okay?" Gulp. "Okay." That night I dug out my plumbing book and memorized the section on septic tanks: sizing separate chambers, flow rates, drainage field layouts, grades and percolation tests, etc. Following the directions in the book, I built a great system and, I am sure, better in many ways than it had to be. My best guess is that it is still working quite well.

One day in the middle of an especially cold Taos winter, I was installing a water pipe for a new gas station. Because the ground, and therefore the water, often freezes in the winter, the pipe needed to be situated deep beneath the surface. That is how I came to be working far enough down in a trench that the sky seemed only a grey slit above me. To make things worse, it had started to sleet, and the wind above was blowing chunks of mud down on me. I was standing in a foot of slush, I was freezing, and I was miserable. I paused for a moment to ponder what I was doing there anyway, and whether this was how the rest of my life would be. After a brief contemplation, I decided, "Yes, if this is how it is going to be, then that is okay with me." It may not have been my first choice, but I was resolved to accept this, or whatever life brought me.

At exactly that moment a co-worker leaned over the ditch and told me, "You might as well quit and climb out, because you are not going to get paid anyway." It seems that the contractor had not only gone broke but had also left town. I contemplated the interesting coincidence of my acceptance just a moment before, and the almost immediate resolution of my present situation. Maybe life had just taught me an important lesson? I reasoned that, having learned it, I was now free to move on. Who really knows? At any rate, my conscience would not permit me to quit without completely assembling the pipe. Then I climbed out of the trench and went to join my fellow workers for coffee in a nice warm café.

I do not think my father ever really understood the reasons for my time spent at the university or my frequent roaming around the country, so this was not a topic we talked about. But he had been a plumber's apprentice as a young man, and worked most of his life as a pipefitter. Our shared occupation in plumbing opened a whole new field of conversation and bonding for us. I know that he was very proud that I was plumbing now and that I had earned the license. He asked questions, such as had I ever calked a joint with oakum, poured hot lead overhead, or sweated a copper joint. I could say yes sometimes, but I also had to tell him that nowadays we used more plastic pipe and different materials. He was curious so we talked about them. It made us both happy.

Of course, today there are newer materials and methods, and I know nothing about them. For that reason, when friends who know I was once a plumber ask for help with a "little problem," I truthfully tell them that when I have a similar problem, I call a plumber.

My mother was amazed that I did **any** manual labor, and that I had built, remodeled, or repaired several of my own houses. Even though I qualified for a plumber's license (which made my father, the ex-plumber happy), my mother remained skeptical. She said she was aware that I knew how to do these things, but that she didn't believe I actually **did** them. She added that I always stood aside and gave directions while other people did the work. No comment. But read on; it gets worse.

BUILDING PROBLEMS

Over the course of several years, I moved back and forth between Taos and Austin, Texas, and I spent quite a bit of time in Mexico as well. At one point, I bought a house in Taos and began to remodel it. As I mentioned in the previous chapter, when my parents visited me, my mother asked me who was doing the work. I said I was. She seemed to try to hide a smile, then she giggled, and next she laughed outright. When she calmed down a bit, she reminded me that I had never been good at, or even before attempted, any construction (whether it be mechanical, electrical, or any other physical work). She did admit that I somehow seemed to have some rudimentary grasp of the concepts but, as she put it, she had never seen me "dirty my hands." She went on to say that despite this, I did have a skill in telling others what to do, and she hated to confess it but, "amazingly, those things usually happened to work out somehow."

I knew what was coming next: the Eddie story. Eddie was my best friend and he was the son of a mechanic. He could actually put things together and make them work. My mother proceeded to tell of the time I stood over poor Eddie for three days, telling him how to build a motorized go-cart, and then (guess), "Who was always the one riding in it?" At least she thought this was probably better than having Eddie push me all the time before I showed him how to install the motor. Enough said, except that I hate to fess up to it, but my mother was right.

The house I was remodeling had been constructed from salvaged railroad ties, which provided thick walls and good insulation but, in accordance with Taos style, the few windows were made as small as those in adobe houses. Late one fall, I purchased a number of old windows from a wreckage yard, and built a greenhouse on one side of the house. After I completed framing them in, I had one huge window left over. I decided that it would provide a wonderful view of Taos Mountain. Hefting my trusty chainsaw, I cut a good-sized hole in the wall. In spite of hitting a nail or two, it was a very satisfying job well done. That is until, less than a half-hour later, a very fast-moving, early snowstorm blew in. Even after I hastily covered the hole with plastic, the wind, snow, and cold blew in for the next week. The wall finally became dry enough for me to install the window, which made a beautiful addition to my living space, and a bittersweet memory.

I seem to have bad luck with weather, or perhaps I have not planned sufficiently. The previous winter, a concrete truck had just delivered a full load of cement when a freeze descended. The floor I was pouring was saved only by a tent of black plastic and big propane heaters. Unpredictable weather? We got it.

The house still stands and I sometimes drive by it. But it is no longer mine and I can't stand to look at it for very long.

I have built many structures over the years, and I check them when I get the opportunity. I want to assure myself that they still work. My children have had to put up with my driving by places, stopping and looking at my still-standing or functioning handiwork, and once again saying, "I built that, you know."

Another of my beautification efforts was the planting of a fresh bed of very expensive imported tulips. Very little of my Dutch heritage remains, but it seems that one gene that persists is the one for growing tulips. I double dug a long trench, mixed manure into the soil and planted the tulips. Then I covered them with straw to protect the bulbs for the winter.

I had forgotten that horses came down from the higher summer elevations in the fall, and the Pueblo owners allowed them to roam around town. The horses happily fed themselves on any available grass, and they had a picnic when they discovered my straw. The tulip bed soon looked as if I just rototilled it. I was by turns saddened, irate, and considering trading my vegetarian diet for horsemeat in retribution.

I related my sad story to a neighbor who grew up in Taos. He said that this was a common problem and I should call the Pueblo and talk to the War Chief (no, I am not making this up). He said the War Chief would see to it that the horses in my yard were removed. The next day two Indians (archaic term but used then) sat in a pick-up truck on the nearby road for several hours. They watched the horses, still in my yard but by now fenced off from the garden. Then the men left, not to return.

My neighbor then told me to again call the War Chief, this time just to be friendly. I should explain that I had caught the horses for them. The only problem was that I had penned them up in a small corral, and, unfortunately, they were totally without food and water. The horses were collected within the hour. In the following spring, several hoof-sized empty spots were visible in my carefully designed array of blooms. Over time, even these filled in and I could begin to laugh about the whole incident. But I learned: I never again used straw, and I kept a lookout for any horses in my yard.

THE PHOTOGENIC HIPPIE

I first came to Taos in the mid-60s. I rode a motorcycle, had long hair and a somewhat unruly beard. Tourists in the plaza apparently viewed me as a good hippie photo opportunity, just as they took photos of the colorful Indians from the pueblo. The Indians would charge the tourists twenty-five or fifty cents whenever they saw a camera pointed at them. I, on the other hand, could never get the photo-happy tourists to shell out even a penny. Somehow, my obviously being Anglo didn't qualify for a fee. I would more likely be told to get a job or a haircut. Most of the tourists looked quite as strange to me--in their shorts, goofy hats and slathered sunblock--as I did to them. Now, of course, I look a lot more like they did then.

Once, a group of young people came through town to proselytize for their church. They were dressed in "hippie" attire for the occasion, but they were way too clean and wholesome looking. They began their spiel by telling how wicked they had been before being saved. I think their greatest sins may have been stealing an extra cookie from the jar, or having an overdue library book, if that. They seemed to think that they needed to establish their bona fides so people would know that they had genuinely changed. Whenever I asked for specifics about their past transgressions, the guys turned hostile and the girls just blushed. I tried to chat up one of these girls, but she was either not interested in me or was more interested in converting me. I observed that none in the group asked what beliefs I already had before they tried to change them. They just assumed their way was better, whatever that may have been. To my mind, they were really quite arrogant in their entire approach.

Perhaps if they had known that I was raised a rigid Calvinist, they might have just given up on me. I would bet that I came from a much more conservative background than they did. Anyway, they were evidently better at sticking to their job than I was at convincing them to try my chosen lifestyle. Maybe I should have taken *their* pictures.

Back then, sitting on a bench in the plaza was a favorite pastime of mine. It should be yours too. There were always lots of interesting things to look at and listen to, and I am sure there still are today. Put aside the camera for a while and take memories with your eyes, ones you can call up anytime, anyplace. As with the memories in this book, many have stayed with me all these years; maybe yours will as well. Make your own stories from what you see and experience right now. If you come to Taos as a tourist and don't observe the swirl of different cultures and fascinating diversity in your midst, you just are not getting your money's worth. If nothing else, sit there and read this book. I feel a desire to share.

One of my great loves in Taos was to spend my day riding my motorcycle in the mountains on twisting highways that hid new scenes behind each bend in the road. I had a wide-angle view unobstructed by the pillars of a car. In addition, with the wind in my face, there were always fragrances to momentarily grab my attention.

When I encountered a particularly fine view or a lingering perfume, it somehow seemed easier to stop the bike than a car. I could even turn around to re-experience whatever caught my attention. I have never found this easy to do in a car.

Searching along secondary roads always drew me forward, even though I had no idea where they might lead, or what adventure I might encounter along the way. As long as there was gas in the tank, I was good. Sometimes when stopping along the way, I met people that took the time to talk for a while. These often-brief encounters added a human touch to my adventures and provided lasting memories. For example, I met a one-armed bartender who showed me a black powder rifle he had made for himself and used in competitions.

Once, a huge brown cow near the roadside took an interest in me. It pushed its way to the closest fence, stuck its wet nose in my face, and mooed loudly when I drove off. Whether this was in regret at my leaving, or a sadness that it could not go with me, I do not know. But I am anthropomorphizing. I do that sometimes.

Another time, a herd of sheep blocked a long stretch of the road as they passed while moving to a new pasture. I still remember the sound and the smell of those sheep. Had I been in a car, I think I would have been annoyed by the delay.

Yet another time, on a very long, straight, two-lane road in the middle of seemingly nowhere, I watched a black cloud filled with lightning and thunder advance upon me. I had no chance of outrunning it. Instead, I slowed down and soon, soaked to my skin, rode whooping and shouting from the sheer joy and wildness of it. Those are memories you can neither plan nor buy.

When my parents visited me, I took each of them on a motorcycle ride on a steep, twisting road leading to a pullout that provided a magnificent view of a green valley far below. Towering mountains surrounded us. Before we climbed back onto the bike, I asked my mother if she was okay. She said yes, that she really enjoyed the ride, and it was something she never thought she would get to do. She said she would brag to the grandchildren about her motorcycle adventure when she got back home.

Next, I took my father for his ride, perhaps a little faster than the previous journey. When we reached the vista, he climbed off the bike, removed his helmet, and in a shaky voice cautioned me, "That was fun but I hope when you took your mother, you went a little slower. She would have been scared." I drove back a lot slower, which he seemed to appreciate. I offered to teach him how to ride the motorcycle, but he declined. My father was an excellent driver of many four-wheel vehicles, but he was not yet ready for the motorcycle. I still have photographs of my parents on the bike together, both looking happy, with my father driving, looking perfectly confident at zero miles per hour. From then on, my parents and I made our excursions in the car.

I gave up the motorcycle a few years later, and for the third time in my life, I had a 1947 Dodge sedan. The first time was when I had a job delivering prescriptions for a drug store. The second time was when I was in the Army and the Dodge was all I could afford. Then I traded it for my first motorcycle, an Indian (and yes, I wish I still had it today). That vehicle did not last long, as within the first week I dropped it in gravel and could not pick it up by myself. I later learned how to do this, but it was too late. The last, or "Taos Dodge," was part nostalgia and part poverty. It was what I was told was a Salesman Special, a coupe long enough that it literally allowed me to fully lie down in the trunk if I chose to do so. It was dark black and I felt like Pa Kettle when driving it. Respectable at last! I never stopped at a gas station, or almost anywhere else, without someone soundly thumping on a fender and proclaiming, "They don't build them like this anymore, no sir." Of all the cars I have owned, I think I loved this one the most.

Somehow, driving around Taos in this car, I felt like a native. Unfortunately, no one ever took my picture in it. However, I do have a photo of the car.

TOMÁS: MI AMIGO

While living in Taos, I acquired some unexpected help with my house and garden, and a new friend. Tomás Morales was a native of Zacatecas, Mexico. He had worked in the United States off and on for more than twenty years. He worked as a beekeeper for a friend of mine, and when the honey was all in and the work ran out, he wanted another job. I did not know it at the time, but I later learned that most of the money he earned was sent home to Mexico each month. It evidently supported not only him and his wife, but almost all of the relatives. His village was twenty miles from the nearest paved road and did not appear on any map I had. Tomás told me that his family survived by raising most of their own food, and selling the little extra they had in order to buy other necessities. There were few opportunities for employment. One of his nieces worked as a waitress, and in order to get to work, she rode a bus an hour each way. Her wages were less than two dollars a day. Any tips she received were very small since the customers were also poor, and she had to share the tips with the cook.

Tomás lived in a spare room in my home, took his meals with me, and was a true friend. He represented a living definition of a strong work ethic. He got up early, and I frequently found him already at work, even before breakfast. If he was not sure what was needed that day, he would chop wood and store it neatly in a pile. Since his

English was very limited, I had to learn to communicate with him in Spanish, which was an added benefit for me. We worked side by side, and when we had to go somewhere, he and my dog Rama sat together in the cab of the truck. *"Nosotros somos cuates,"* he said of us. "Buddies." When we went to buy lumber or other supplies, we would stop at the grocery store and each buy a few candy bars to eat on the way. We shared this "secret sin" together. We would occasionally clean the truck of wrappers because others might otherwise laugh at us, or worse, want us to share. The only "fault" I could find with him was that I could hardly keep him in jalapeños. One week he ate an entire institutional-sized can of them. With this, I could live.

When he left, what I missed most about him was his laugh, even though it was sometimes at my expense. He helped me by correcting my Spanish, for example, but more often he just shook his head and laughed. I tried to tell him that his Spanish was Mexican Spanish, but my Spanish was from New Mexico and it was the REAL Spanish. He was not buying it. And by the way, as I mentioned earlier, you would be safer to refer to the people in New Mexico as Spanish, not Mexican. Here the language and lineage go back hundreds of years to Spain.

I promised Tomás that I would visit him in Mexico. He was skeptical and obliquely expressed his doubt that I would do this. *"Señor,"* he said, "my village is so small it will be difficult for you to find. And besides, what will we feed you? I know that you do not eat meat." Then suddenly, as if an idea had just struck him, he slyly said,

"I know! If you visit, my wife will cook hay for you. You can eat that!" And together we roared with laughter. But I did visit him, and I did not eat hay, but wonderful meatless foods prepared by his wife.

Before Tomás left the United States, he wanted to visit a relative who lived in California, but the only way for him to get there was by airplane. To go by bus took too long, and the routes were too complicated. He was in this country legally; however, we didn't want him to have any problems with his papers. For the trip, he bought a nice suit, tie, dress shoes, and luggage at a Goodwill store. He had his hair cut and mustache trimmed. Although he spoke almost no English, that was not a problem. Spanish was often a common language and, of course, there was no intense security screening at that time. When Tomás got on the plane, he looked like an ambassador: regal and dignified, a man that no one would question as to legality. I wish I had taken more pictures. If there had been cell phones back then, I am sure we would have an album full of photos.

Tomás found work elsewhere the following year, so I did not see him, but I went to visit him in Mexico in the fall, as promised. He was right about the village being difficult to find, and he had underestimated both the length of the road leading to it, and the number of ruts it contained. Having sent him a letter beforehand, he knew I was coming and so, it seemed, did everyone else who lived there. That far back in the tules, I was possibly the first Anglo most of the people had seen, either in the village or anywhere. A huge celebration had been prepared, and I think that everyone had been invited or just wandered over to see me. Introductions that began at first with timid handshakes soon became warm *abrazos*. Everything I ate was delicious and each time there was a new offering, I was assured that it did not contain meat. "But does it contain hay?" I would ask. Everyone knew the joke, and everyone laughed.

It seemed they had also been told a story of how I helped Tomás purchase a semi-legal, or as they smilingly called it, a "wetback" truck that somehow had been transferred across the border. They told me with gratitude how much they appreciated this vehicle and how it benefited the whole village. Of course, they added that whenever the *Federales* came around, they had to hide it in the bushes since officially it didn't exist. And, of course, it did **not** exist, and I hadn't done anything to help them, and I will deny it to this day.

Of all the people I met that day, I remember the children the best. Many times, I wondered how difficult it must be to grow up so poor, but I saw that they were as loved and cared for as any children I have ever met. Each child wanted to be picked up by me and kissed for good luck.

The only moment of slight embarrassment was when I asked for the toilet. "*Excusado*? *Necesario*?" I tried. There was no response. I wondered if I had somehow used an impolite word. Tomás exchanged worried looks with his wife. Then Tomás whispered in my ear, "Over there among the cactus, *Señor*. You will see the newspaper." "It's okay," I reassured him, and headed off.

Both Tomás and his wife encouraged me to spend the night with them, but having seen their small home with only one bedroom, I made excuses and said that I was expected elsewhere. I knew that if I slept in the bed, they would have had to sleep on the dirt floor.

Upon leaving, it seemed that the entire population once more lined up to say goodbye. Many villagers I had not even formally met gave me firm hugs, and often had tears in their eyes. It is embarrassing, but they made it seem that they were the ones who felt honored that a gringo had come to their village. In truth, it was my honor to be with them, and one of the happiest and wonderful memories that I carry with me. I know that I smiled the entire time I was writing this, and might even have had a tear in my eye as I remembered.

CELIA'S PLACE

In 1970 I lived in the Casa Carlos, a building on Governor Bent Street that had been unoccupied for several years. Carmen, who owned it, rented me a room there, but she assured me that it was only because someone else had vouched for me. Taoseños are very particular about who they deal with and, in this case, she would have rather let the property remain vacant than allow someone she did not know occupy it. Without the introduction, the fact that I had long hair, a beard, and asked her where I could park my motorcycle probably would not have gone in my favor. The rent was low, but it took me two days just to clean the room. I was later to discover who some of the previous tenants had been.

When I lived there, all the other rooms in the building were empty. My room was downstairs. The bathroom was upstairs and down a hallway. It had a balcony, and if I liked, I could sit in the tub and look out the window onto the street. Unfortunately, my bed also faced the street, just where there was a little jog in the road. There was quite a bit of traffic on this street, especially late at night when at least some percentage of the drivers were likely to be drunk. And, since the building partially blocked the street, vehicles had to make a slight jog there. I lived in mortal fear as vehicles drove toward me, racing through the chicane with their headlights shining directly into the window of my room. More than once it occurred to me that if only one drunk missed the bend in the road one time, their car or truck would end up in bed with me. Nevertheless, I was very happy living there and I retain fond memories of the place.

The last time I visited Taos, there was a restaurant in the building and my old room was a dining area, first door on the left. I am told that the building has had several other incarnations before and since, but currently it is "Lambert's of Taos."

There is a rather stupid game that kids played when I was young. They would call people several times a night to ask questions like, "Is Bob there?" and then hang up. After an hour or so of this, and when the victim was thoroughly annoyed, the last caller would begin with "Hello, this is Bob. Are there any messages for me?"

Hang on; there is a point to this story. I was initially unaware of the previous usage of my building. I occasionally received a knock on my door, and when I answered it, a man would always ask if Celia lived there. The callers always seemed quite disappointed when I told them that I was the only tenant, and had no idea who Celia was or where she might have gone. One day--did you see this coming? -- someone knocked and when I answered, a youngish and attractive woman said, "Hi, my name is Celia. I used to live here."

At my invitation Celia entered, looked around, and since I had only one chair, she sat herself quite comfortably on the bed. She asked a number of questions about me and suddenly with a smile purred, "Hey, I think you're kind of cute." I felt quite uncomfortable about her possible motives (okay, I'm a square sometimes). I quickly asked if we might go for coffee, i.e., go somewhere else. However, she just smiled at me and said no, that she was just passing through, and it was nice meeting me. She said that she just wanted to see the place again and relive a few old memories. The last thing she said was, "That bed was mine, you know." Then she was out of the door and into the night. That, at least for me, seemed to answer one question, and raised a number of others.

I have been told recently by friends that my old home is sometimes currently referred to as "a one-time bordello." Times **have** changed, haven't they?

I'm certain that Celia was only one of several past occupants. While cleaning the room, I discovered a clue about two other prior tenants. Penciled on the window ledge was the inscription, "Jorge Luis loves Maria Lucas." Beneath this was written their addresses. Let me admit it: I am a romantic at heart. I imagined Jorge writing his declaration of love, and writing their addresses, even to the zip codes, to seal the relationship. Recording the bond in this way would make it more official, almost like a marriage vow.

The next notation was in a different script, probably that of Maria. It completed the closing chapter of their love story with the dates of Jorge's birth and then his death, and the fact that he was buried in Taos, New Mexico on November 18, 1967. It is my own fantasy, but I have always considered this a beautiful, if very sad, love poem. Here were two people with perhaps limited education and opportunity who were expressing themselves as best they could. Even today as I write this, it brings a tear to my eyes. So many years later and still, to me, it is a poignant view into the lives of those people I never knew.

DOG TROUBLE

Maybe you already know this, but if you are visiting Taos and have your dog with you, the dog might find some of the many chickens, sheep, cows, and horses new to them. These farm animals sometimes wander about freely, and if your dog is not restrained, it may take off to investigate. The animals run, the dog chases. You get the picture. Dogs sometimes become lost this way, or other bad things happen.

One time I was listening to a sheepherder and his neighbor who asked him how things were going. "Oh, fine," he said, "I just got done selling a bunch of sheep, and did really good, too." "How so?" "Well, the ones I sold at market did okay, but the one I sold to the tourist whose dog killed it, went for almost five hundred dollars!" "Really?" "Yeah, it was some very special sheep breed, and a prize-winning show animal, you know. When I told the guy that, he was just glad to pay and get out of there before I called the sheriff."

Then there are people whose heads and hearts are definitely lacking something. When they no longer want a pet, they just dump it somewhere and leave. Many of the animals do not last long by themselves, but sometimes dogs revert to their feral state and form packs, just as their ancestors did. At their worst, these dogs can even be dangerous to humans; usually they just go through garbage cans or attack smaller wild or domestic animals in order to survive, but not always.

My neighbor Sam called me one afternoon and told me to keep my dog in for a few nights. He had a small herd of cattle nearby, and recently a pack of dogs chased them every night. These dogs often ran the animals ragged or bunched them up so that they could not eat. He said a few of the cows had also been nipped at their heels badly and were almost crippled. He wanted me to know that for the next few nights he would be "thinning those dogs out a bit."

I did hear gunshots for a few evenings and guessed that Sam was making good on his war against the wild dog pack. When I next saw him, I asked how it had gone. He replied, "Pretty good," and he didn't reckon that the few remaining dogs would come around again for a while. Then he laughed and told me a story. He said that when he called another neighbor of ours to warn her to keep her poodle indoors, she told him that he had no right to shoot dogs, that he had always been a bad person, and that she was thinking about calling the sheriff to report him. Then with a big smile, he told me that the woman called yesterday and asked if he was still shooting those dogs. He replied affirmatively, and she said in a great deal of anger, "Well, Sam, I hope you get every damn one of them! They killed my poor Daisy last night." Then he just shook his head and said he guessed it all depended on whose ox was being gored, didn't it?

RAMA: LOVE OF MY LIFE

The discussion in the previous chapter regarding the dumping of animals was particularly relevant to me because my dog had been abandoned. One cold winter, I found him sleeping in the warmth of my compost heap. At first, he ran when he saw me. As I became more familiar to him, he stopped running from me. Instead, he would stay and watch me, as if he was trying to make up his mind. When I began to leave food out for him, he slowly came a little closer. One day he finally let me pet him, and on one especially bad night, I let him sleep inside in the warmth of my greenhouse. He became my dog. He was a large German Shepherd mix, and I named him Rama. I do not know what happened to him before we met, but from then on, he seldom left my side. Everyone believes that their dog, or child, is special but all I can say is that he was special to me. I enjoyed each moment of our relationship until the time he died. Those of you who have loved an animal know what I mean. Even as I think of him now and write this, it is with a mixture of joy and sadness. I never wanted another dog after him; maybe that has been a loss for both me and a new dog.

Rama especially loved to ride in the back of my truck. He went almost everywhere I went, and when told to stay, he always patiently waited until my return. He usually knew when I was going somewhere, and he would run to the truck waiting expectantly to find out whether he would be riding in the back or in the cab. One day I could not take him with me, and I told him that he would have to stay home. This news would usually occasion a spectacular display of guilt induction, with him moping and begging, but this time he seemed to calmly accept my decision. He slowly walked back to the shade where he had been sitting, and with never even a whimper, he stayed there. At last, I thought; I have finally shown him who the boss is here. When I left the house, he was still lying under a tree, seemingly content to be left behind. He didn't even look at me.

I took my usual route (one he knew well) to the main highway, about a mile from the house. I stopped for a yield sign and waited for traffic to thin out so I could turn. Suddenly, Rama burst out from some bushes, leaped into the truck bed, and stood there panting. Or was that a smile on his face? Clearly, he had cut across the fields and had run furiously to beat me to this spot. Obviously, he knew that from where I was in the truck, I could not see him until it was too late. We looked at one another. To me, he looked very satisfied with himself, and maybe a little amused by his joke on me. I looked a little annoyed but probably equally amused by his cleverness. What happened next? Well, I knew that letting him go with me might reinforce what could have become a bad behavior, and I should not have let him get by with it, but I had to take him with me. Secretly, I was actually quite proud of him. What a smart dog I had.

I once stopped at a Dairy Queen, and it being a hot day, I returned with an ice cream cone for Rama. Thereafter he would bark and get excited whenever he saw a Dairy Queen. This is what we psychologists call "One Trial Learning." I frequently did reinforce this behavior as well with ice cream cones for each of us. Pavlov would have loved Rama.

Once I had to go out of town for a week. When I returned, Rama happened to be on a second-floor porch as I walked up to the house. To my horror, when he saw me, he jumped from the height, scrambled a bit when he landed, and then took the straightest course to me. Unfortunately, this happened to be right through the open doors of a car from which its surprised occupants were just then getting out. Fortunately, they were very kind people, did not get upset, and just laughed as they watched him climb all over me and slobber me with dog kisses.

Rama was usually a very gentle dog and I seldom even heard him growl, but at times it was clear that he was still a Shepherd and had built-in instincts as a protector. Kids could crawl all over him and pull his ears, but he would never even get testy with them. Instead, he would look to me imploringly as if to say, "Please, get them off of me." However, there was one time when he demonstrated his true potential.

I usually do not answer the door when it is clear that the visitor is trying to sell something. On this occasion, I was perhaps mildly interested in the product, or I was being unusually polite, and I let this man in to demonstrate his wares. It very soon became apparent that he was obnoxious. I had grown tired of his spiel and was ready for him to leave. I firmly told him that I was not interested after all, and he would be wasting both my time and his if he continued. At this, he unwisely decided to force the issue by trying to push a bunch of unwanted material on me. He suddenly stood up and made a quick move in my direction. Rama immediately leaped off the ground, with jaws open, toward the salesman. Only a quick command from me halted Rama and saved the man from a very nasty experience. The shaken salesperson quickly left. Rama lay on the floor looking disappointed. To me, his eyes seemed to register both a lost opportunity and his question of whether he had done the right thing. I assured him he was a wonderful companion and I appreciated him, but in the future maybe he should wait until I asked him to rescue me.

This was not the only time that Rama made an independent assessment of a situation or a person and acted upon it. Of course, I couldn't be sure that the decision was always uniquely his own, or in response to whatever he picked up from feelings I was projecting. A young man who lived next door to me often played his music too loudly. In the daytime, a simple phone call would suffice to tone it down, until the next time he was drinking or "just forgot."

One night, he returned home drunk, flipped on his stereo and passed out with the speakers going full blast. Of course, he was either too asleep or too deafened to answer the phone. The next morning, I went to his yard to talk with him once more about the problem. This time I was most certainly still visibly annoyed. He acted properly abashed, and agreed that I had a perfect right to be upset, and he swore it wouldn't happen again. Just then, I noticed Rama expressing his own disapproval of the man, which he was pointedly demonstrating with a lifted leg. I quickly left with a parting, "Don't let it happen again."

When I told this story to friends, they, of course, loved it. And after they finished laughing, they offered to take bets on how long it took, if ever, for the man to notice his soaked trousers.

Good Dog!

THE MOUSE

Y ou might think that adobe walls nearly eighteen-inches thick would keep out most insects and other pests, but they do not. I suppose the invaders find the advantages of comfortable living as attractive as I do, and what is more, there are so many places to hide. So it went with a little mouse that became, if not my friend, at least my housemate.

It began one winter evening when I was reading. I heard a slight rustling noise, but I could not ascertain an immediate cause for it. So I went back to my reading, until I heard it again. I got up and looked around, and still nothing. The next night I was again reading when I heard the noise, but this time its source suddenly appeared in plain sight, scampering along a shelf in my kitchen: a mouse. As I looked, this little grey thing stopped, lifted its head and, I swear, looked directly at me. We seemed to both have the same question in our minds, "What are **you** doing here?"

With a little detective work, I discovered that a box of grain had a neat hole nibbled into its side and a thin flow of seeds coming from it. This could not continue! The next day, I bought a Have-A-Heart trap, baited it, and waited for my mouse to "Come and get it!" It came, it sniffed, it went into the wire mesh trap, grabbed the bait, and went out again. Hmmm. It seemed that a little reworking of the trigger mechanism was in order. The next night, the same thing happened: the mouse moved in and out, nibbling my cheese. A clever mouse; so let the battle begin!

I rigged the trap with a long string so that as soon as the mouse entered, I could release the trapdoor myself. Enter mouse, pull string and *voilà*, I had it. "It" because I never did figure out whether the mouse was male or female. I took the cage and mouse out to some nearby bushes, explained that I was sure it would be much happier there, opened the door and left. Good job, Alexander!

You, of course, have already have guessed that the story does not end here. The very next night, a mouse was there again, but could I be sure that this was the same mouse? Since the mouse was being very cooperative, I repeated the performance of baiting and trapping. Since I am a scientist well versed in doing research, I dabbed a little spot of red paint on its head before once more letting it escape. But this time, I took it much further (about a city block) from the house. Just by looking at the writing below, you already know that this story is still not over, don't you?

As if it could tell time, the mouse returned on the next night, replete with its red dot, and looking hungry from its long trip home. It seemed to me that I had only two choices at this juncture, one having a much less Have-a-Heart ending to it. I cleaned the food shelf and moved everything from gnawable containers into metal ones. I stocked up on some healthy mouse treats, and put out at least one each night. When I was gone for several days, a friend came and fed my guest. Softie.

I soon began to look forward to the evening visits by my new buddy. I do not know where it stayed during the day. I did look, but there was an abundance of hiding places. It could have been anywhere, and maybe I really did not want to know. I enjoyed its presence and thought perhaps it enjoyed mine. I brought it special treats once in a while, or at least what I thought might be special treats to an omnivorous mouse.

One night it didn't show up, and I never saw it again. Maybe it decided to live outside when the weather warmed up, maybe it went looking for a mate, or maybe a cat got it, or…. I don't know.

The mouse was gone and, to be truthful, it left a vacant spot in my day, and maybe even in my heart. Do I still think about it? Well, I **am** writing about it, am I not? Next is a small indulgence of mine. Perhaps your kids will find it amusing, or not. But here it is; feel free to tear the page out if you like.

The Mouse in My House

A little mouse came into my house
And I surely wished it would go out
But it did not play so fair with me
It ran from here and it ran to there
It seemed that it was everywhere
Even tried to make my house a lair

Since it seemed it would not leave
Even though I nicely asked it please
I set a trap for it, a little cage
And baited it with tasty cheese
I soon caught that little mouse
And then I took it from the house

Soft, sweet, nice, cuddly little mouse
You are very, very cute I know
But I really do not want you here
You can maybe live some other place
Perhaps go and even start a family
With spouse and kids somewhere

But please don't ever come back here
For I really do not want you near
My house is only made for people
Not mice or snakes or spiders either
I like it fine with just my book and I
So now goodbye and don't return!

LAST COMMENT

Well, of course, there are many more stories from my Taos days: tales of communes, of meeting a guru, of friendships and love, and a few things I think I will keep to myself. But they will have to wait for a lengthier and personal discussion, over a bottle of wine and beside a Taos fireplace, I hope.

Namaste.

Made in the USA
Lexington, KY
25 November 2019